NOTES FROM A
PANDEMIC

NOTES FROM A
PANDEMIC

~ A Journal of the Plague Year ~

ELIZABETH SAITO

For more information about this title, contact the publisher:

Elizabeth Saito
elizabeth.saito@gmail.com

Additional copies of this book can be
purchased through Eight Cousins Books:
189 Main Street, Falmouth, MA
508-548-5548
eightcousins.com

ISBN: 978-0-9981768-5-7

Printed in the United States of America by IngramSpark

Cover Design by Van-garde Imagery, Inc.
Cover Art by Scott Ruescher
Interior design: Van-garde Imagery, Inc.

For Makoto, Kunio & Rory

Acknowledgments

Versions of these essays originally appeared as near-weekly columns in the *Falmouth Enterprise* from March 2020 until April 2021. I am grateful to publisher Bill Hough for giving my work a home.

My sincerest thanks to all those who have guided and encouraged me these past two years: Rebecca Hayden, Scott Ruescher, Parimal Patil, Rebecca Goldstein, Ben Roth, Micah Trautmann, John Gibson, Molly Bang, Jon Franzen, and Eric Edwards.

Contents

MARCH 2020

    Social Starvation 1

APRIL 2020

    On Gratitude 3

    Wishful Thinking 5

    Looking Closely 7

MAY 2020

    This Land is My Land 11

    The Desiring Heart 15

    On Relatives and Rituals 19

JUNE 2020

    Land of the White 23

    My Mental Troubles 27

    I'll Have the Unusual 31

    On Beauty 35

JULY 2020

On Poetry and Prayer 39

Remotely Learning 45

No Screen Time without Clean Time 49

AUGUST 2020

Masks Up! 53

Can't You Count Them? 57

On Routines 61

SEPTEMBER 2020

Turns in the Weather 65

Remoter Parenting 69

Dreaming during a Pandemic 73

OCTOBER 2020

You're Doing the Right Thing 75

Essential 79

The Procreant Urge 83

NOVEMBER 2020

On Small-town Politics 87

Profit Margin 91

DECEMBER 2020

COVID's Cairns 95

On Death 99

Digital Christmas .103

JANUARY 2021

Anti-Social Media .107

On Zooming 111

FEBRUARY 2021

    Mind Your Mask 115

    What's Wrong with This Picture? 119

    On the Merits of Gruesome Fairy Tales 121

MARCH 2021

    Past Plagues 127

    Darkness and Light 131

APRIL 2021

    Let There Be Light 133

NOVEMBER 2021

    Epilogue. 135

Social Starvation

March 2020

At Shaw's the other day, I got in line behind an older gentleman with a kindly look. "Not very crowded today," he observed.

"I was here the day schools closed," I replied. "The lines went all the way back to the meat department. No bananas, no eggs. Toilet paper? Forget it."

Apparently, both of us had just been down the frozen pizza aisle. "I've been doing some market research," he said, "and I don't think cauliflower-crust pizza is very popular."

It had indeed been hilarious: the entire freezer had been wiped out—except for towers of cauliflower crust pizza.

"Yeah, who eats that stuff? Even in a pandemic, no one wants it."

The man left and I was up next at the register. The woman bagging my groceries had a harried look. "Is it a struggle to get to work?" I asked. "Do you have kids at home?"

"My kids are grown."

"I really appreciate you coming to work, helping us all stay fed."

"You're welcome," she replied wearily.

That job must be so stressful right now: repeated exposure in close proximity to strangers, strangers desperate for a chat on their week's one and only outing from the house.

On Gratitude

April 2020

Against the current backdrop of helplessness and fear, I find small victories worth celebrating.

The other night, I was having trouble falling asleep. I usually put my watch on top of the dresser, but that night I'd laid it on the bedside table, and its ticking was irritating. Getting out of bed felt like more than I could manage, so instead I took a wool sock that was also on the bedside table and stuffed the watch inside to muffle the ticking.

The next morning, I swiped the dirty clothes from around our bedroom and loaded them in the washer. Ten minutes later, when I went to put on my watch, I realized it was now swishing around in the warm soapy water. Running down to the basement, I lifted the lid, stuck my hand in, and felt about as the center agitator lurched around, indifferent to my plight. Grasping something promising, I fished it up: behold, the watch, still snuggled inside the sock—still ticking!

My last hair tie had broken the day before. Walking in the woods, I spied one half buried in the dirt. Normally I'd have walked right by, but as I'm avoiding stores like the plague (*because* of the plague), this was my chance to defer a need. I picked it up, brushed it off, and wrapped it around my hair.

On a gray morning, I was walking along Quissett Harbor's western beach. The wind was blowing out of the harbor, pushing little ripples along the sandy shoreline. I increased my speed to a slow trot, matching the speed of the ripples. We were flowing along, the ripples and I, when a submerged pair of bright-blue child's sunglasses came suddenly into view. My five-year-old loves wearing sunglasses (even indoors), and so I stopped, rolled up my sleeve, and fished them out. A tiny slipper shell had attached itself to the right lens.

My brother, who's been laid off from his job, was doing some spring raking and found a one-dollar bill in his leaf pile. Sometimes it doesn't take much to feel lucky.

Wishful Thinking

April 2020

After roasting a chicken, I set the wishbone on the kitchen windowsill to dry and, a few days later, explained the game to my five-year-old, Rory. "We both make a wish, and whoever breaks off the larger piece, their wish will come true!" I then strategically offered him what looked like the stronger bone.

Not realizing that wishes are supposed to be made silently, he said, "I wish to be able to do whatever I want."

I said, "I wish for our family and friends to be safe from the virus."

Rory's side snapped off along with the node where the two bones fuse. Delight, and then a shade of disbelief, passed over his face. "I get to do whatever I want?"

"Depends. What do you want to do?"

"Watch a video!"

He headed off to get the iPad, then stopped, turned round, and came back. "Actually Mommy, I wish for both of our wishes to come true."

Looking Closely

April 2020

On a sunny, windy morning, I was walking along Vineyard Sound just west of Trunk River, where the beach is all stones. The surf was up, and I settled my distracted mind on listening to the shushing, scurried sound of the waves rattling the stones as they receded. On my way back to our house, I walked through Spohr Gardens, stopping to touch and smell the pink flowers of the early blooming azaleas. I'm glad this pandemic hit in the spring, of all seasons, its beauty and expansiveness an antidote to the contraction and fear.

I've recently begun memorizing poetry while out walking (another way to settle a distracted mind) and am drawn right now to Mary Oliver, a longtime resident of Provincetown, who died just over a year ago. Oliver's poetry combines deftly crafted observations of the natural world with an openness to its mercilessness and the inevitability of death. Her poem "The Black Snake" tells the story of seeing a truck in front of her run over a snake. She stops the car. The snake's body is now "looped and useless as an old bicycle tire." She carries the snake—"cool and gleaming as a braided wipe"—and lays it under some bushes by the side of the road. Getting back in her car, she drives on, thinking about death, "[i]ts suddenness, its terrible weight, its certain coming." The poem concludes:

> *Yet under*
> *reason burns a brighter fire, which the bones*
> *have always preferred.*
> *It is the story of endless good fortune.*
> *It says to oblivion: not me!*
> *It is the light at the center of every cell.*
> *It is what sent the snake coiling and flowing*
> *   forward*
> *happily all spring through the green leaves before*
> *   he came to the road.*

The other day, on a walk down to Quissett Harbor, I ran into a neighbor who told me her son had all the symptoms of COVID-19—high fever, aches, cough—but there were no tests available to confirm the infection. This neighbor is also a Mary Oliver fan, and she told me that when her mother was in the hospital a few months ago, she'd sat beside her and read to her for hours from a volume of Oliver's poems. Standing there, much farther apart than felt natural, with a mid-tide lapping at the harbor's stone wall, I recited "The Black Snake" to my neighbor.

When I find myself sinking into anxiety, grasping for new structures, bereft of the old ones, the best thing I can do for myself is take a walk, find some sign of spring, anything—a robin yanking up worms, the electric green of the moss on a wet day, the lengthening spears of the beech leaves—and just look at it, closely.

This Land is My Land

May 2020

Something happened this past Mother's Day that really pissed me off. I'd just delivered a vase of tulips and daffodils picked from our yard on Ransom Road to my mother, who lives around the corner on Sippewissett Road. It was around 7:30 PM, and I could see that it was going to be a spectacular sunset, so instead of driving straight home, I decided to drive up Racing Beach Avenue to enjoy the view west over Buzzards Bay.

Racing Beach is a private neighborhood, but I've been walking there for years. When my first son was little, I'd go several times a week to push his stroller up and down that beautiful coastal road. There is a large "Private: No Trespassing" sign posted at the entrance to the neighborhood, but I got to know an older gentleman, Mort, who lived on the corner next to the sign, and he assured me I was welcome. Mort was often out in his yard when I strolled by, and we'd have a chat. I got a tour of his camper van and learned all about grandchildren; one Christmas, he and his wife, Sue, invited our family over to eat homemade rum balls.

When I drove up to the entrance this Mother's Day, a new sign was posted: "Beach Parking Prohibited During the COVID-19 Emergency." Admittedly, I should have turned around. But instead, I thought, "I'm not *parking* at the beach; I'm just going to stop my car for a few minutes to enjoy the view." As I drove down to the ocean, I noticed that many of the huge houses normally deserted this time of year had lights on and cars in the driveway: the one percent, sheltering in their country homes. Reaching the coastal road, I pulled over, and had been there less than a minute when a sleek, black Lexus pulled up beside me. The driver, a man in his late fifties perhaps, rolled down his window. I rolled down my passenger window.

"Do you live here?" he asked aggressively.

My back up instantly, I felt like saying, "Yeah, I live here year-round. *Do you*?"

Instead, I said, "I live on Ransom Road."

"Ransom, huh," he said, as if he'd really got me now. "Do you have beach rights? You're trespassing."

I didn't say anything. I just looked at him.

"You need to leave, now."

Ransom Road is a private dead-end street, but there's a footpath off the cul-de-sac that leads through the woods to Spohr Gardens and from there down to the bike path. We get a lot of walkers and cyclists on our street who do not live on it, almost certainly some of them from Racing Beach. At road association meetings, the option to post a "No Trespassing" sign frequently comes up. The road has a nearly ninety-degree blind turn at the bottom of a hill, which cyclists sometimes take at breakneck speed, and the boogie man of liability "if anything ever happened" rears its head. I've always been opposed to cutting off public access; politically, it rubs me the wrong way. Instead, we have signs that read, "Private Road: Travel with Care," and, "Slow: Curve Ahead."

I was technically breaking the law, but there's a polite way to tell someone to leave your neighborhood, and an impolite way to do it. Perhaps this man had spent his whole day kindly shooing foreigners off the street, and by sunset, his civility had been used up. But the whole interaction just felt so alpha-male, as if he relished flexing his property rights. On Mother's Day, no less!

The Desiring Heart

May 2020

My son Rory couldn't be happier to be home all day. He doesn't miss preschool or trips to the playground or trips to the library or trips anywhere. He's content tinkering with Lego, bouncing on the trampoline, and roaming the yard pretending he's Luke Skywalker. But my sanity depends on getting away from the house and its Sisyphean housework.

A few weekends ago, my husband and I were able to coax Rory off our property for a bike ride to the Knob, the hooked spit of conservation land that shelters Quissett Harbor, where, under an azure sky, we spent the afternoon investigating the tide pools among the rocks at the north end of the Knob's western shore. Before we'd even left the beach, I was anxious to repeat the experience.

And so for the next two weeks, I tried in vain to lure him back there, with cookies, with ultimatums, with frustrated begging. Once, he relented, and I—so excited—got the tandem bike out of the garage. But then he refused to get on it. "I am *not* going to the Knob!" What's wrong with my child, I fumed.

We allow our boys two hours a day to play video games, time that I use to do yoga, meditate, and write— or, sometimes, to do yoga, meditate, and then stand morosely in the middle of our living room, overwhelmed by the clutter, the triangle Rory drew on the couch cushion, the crumbs dug into the rug, the dust bunnies socializing in the corner. This sense of joyless domestic servitude is harder to combat when you've been advised by the governor to stay inside your house all day every day with your two children.

For the past two years, I've been learning to meditate through an online tutorial and have just finished a unit on managing stress. The teacher guides you through the technique—where you visualize your body filling up with a warm, spacious light—and then leaves you with some parting thoughts to consider. One day, he said, "Stress arises when we want things to be different than they are."

With the weather warming, Rory has been willing to leave the yard to go kayaking on the pond just down the road from our house. He rides in his child's flat-top kayak while I orbit around in an adult one we borrowed from a neighbor (ours has a leak). But I couldn't let go of wanting to repeat that afternoon we'd spent at the Knob, and so I decided to try a different approach. When Rory woke up—prepared not to get my way—I went in and snuggled him and said, "I have a desire in my heart today, Rory."

"What is it?"

"My heart's desire is to go to the Knob."

He said he didn't want to go to the Knob. I got up to make breakfast. A minute later he called out from the bedroom, "Mommy! We can do your heart's desire. We can go to the Knob."

After breakfast, I got the bike out of the garage, got his helmet on, and then he said, "Actually, Mommy, I don't want to go to the Knob." Unlike the week before, I didn't feel like kicking anything. A moment later, he chirped, "Let's go kayaking!"

This time of year, the rim of the pond is laden with baby painted turtles sunning themselves on rocks and half-submerged branches. Rory and I love sneaking up on them. There can be a dozen or more piled on one rock, and when you draw close, they flee, their bright orange-yellow undershells bumping and clattering against the stone before they slide beneath the surface, where, graceful once more, they swim down out of sight.

The southern edge of our property slopes steeply into wooded conservation land. A few days ago, I was clearing a path from our house down into the forest, making excellent headway through a thicket of bull brier when Rory came over and proposed kayaking.

"Rory, it's my heart's desire to keep working on this path."

He came over and wrapped his arms around my legs. "Come down."

I knelt beside him and he put his ear to my chest. "Mommy, I can hear your heart's desire: it's to go kayaking."

I embraced him, my eyes closed. "You're my heart's desire."

On Relatives and Rituals

May 2020

Rory and I were planting tomatoes when, apropos of nothing, he asked, "Who was the first person? Where did people come from?"

"In the beginning," I told him, "there was no life on earth. No plants. No animals. Just the ocean, the wind, rain, rocks, and chemicals. Then those chemicals mixed together and somehow a tiny speck of a creature came into being. Just a single cell. No eyes, no ears. Then that tiny creature got more complicated and multiplied into different creatures, with ears and eyes, and feelings, and eventually there were lots of big animals, including chimpanzees, which are like monkeys. And very slowly some of those monkeys turned into humans. So your great-great-

great-great-great-great-great-great-great-way-back-grandparents were monkeys."

Rory listened but didn't say anything. I wasn't sure how much of the creation story he'd absorbed, and so I recapped, "All life is descended from a tiny creature that came alive when nothing else was. And humans came from monkeys."

A few days later, Memorial Day, I told Rory we were going to the cemetery in Woods Hole to meet up with Grandma at the grave of his great-great-great-grandparents. He looked up, curious, a little alarmed, and asked, "Were they like monkeys?"

The theory of evolution laid waste to a story that structured believers' relation to their God for millennia, and this pandemic has laid waste to countless routines that structured our days, weeks, and years. Life feels out of joint; there's no hand-hold, no pattern to follow.

My mother and her sister have a tradition of visiting their parents' grave in Maine every Memorial Day, but my aunt is stuck in Hawaii (all commercial flights are cancelled) and my mom didn't want to do the long drive without her, and so she enlisted me as her substitute grave companion. As we stood there at the tombstones—the only (living) people on the property—a sedan drove up the cemetery's dirt road. An older couple and an elderly woman got out and walked in our direction, coming to a stop at the same graves we were gathered round. Who were these people?

The elderly woman, Marilyn Young, was the wife of my mother's father's cousin, and the man, her son, Robert Young, was my mother's second cousin, whom she had not seen since she was a girl. We'd been only vaguely aware of these relatives when various forces pulled us back to this place where some of our ancestors lay buried. My mother had called Robert when she'd moved to town; they'd talked about getting together, but a plan had never materialized.

My great-great-grandparents, Grace and Josiah Young, were administrators at the leper colony founded on Penikese Island at the turn of the century. This much I knew. But I now learned which house on North Street my great-great-grandmother ran as a boarding house when she and Josiah left Penikese for Woods Hole. And I learned that Marilyn Young's mother, Maybelle Rockwell, lived in the house at the top of Ransom Road, the street I now live on. I learned that Robert Young has a son named Gregory, my brother's name. I learned all this because my mom and her sister didn't go to Maine, as they do every year, on Memorial Day.

Land of the White

June 2020

On Wednesday, my family and I joined in the Black Lives Matter march in Woods Hole, where hundreds of marchers calling for an end to police brutality against Black Americans made their way up Water Street and then around Eel Pond. Many marchers held signs; all of them—without exception—wore face masks.

I belong to Falmouth's Unitarian-Universalist Fellowship, where our minister preaches often about "the beloved community." The beloved community was a vision of society championed by Martin Luther King Jr., a society in which equity flows from radical, inclusive love. The march was a call to realize that vision.

My ancestry is a mix of Irish and English. My husband was born in our nation's capital to a Scottish mother and a Japanese father. A few months ago, he was standing at the Sagamore bus stop when he and the white guy next to him began talking. When asked what he did for work, my husband said he was an oceanographer, and the man, impressed, said, "You Asians are so smart—not like us Americans." The man had meant well—he'd been trying to pay my husband a compliment—but instead he'd reinforced a racial stereotype as well as the idea that to be American is to be white. Something like this has never happened to me; it's inconceivable that my race would ever usurp my citizenship.

I grew up in a nearly all-white suburb of Boston, and I had the privilege of growing up without giving my race much thought. It's embarrassing that it's taken me decades to realize this is an exclusively white privilege. The education I received about the civil rights movement in this suburb's elite public school read like an incomprehensible Disney version of social change. My American history teacher loved to emphasize that "the civil war wasn't fought over slavery. It was fought to keep the union together." And why, exactly, was the nation ripping apart?

It wasn't until my mid-20s, when I read a historically annotated volume of Martin Luther King Jr.'s speeches, that I came to understand the brutality and terrorism that enforced segregation, to understand that King's assassination wasn't an isolated act by a crazed individual, but that King had in fact foreseen a violent end to his life in his final speech in Memphis. "Like anybody, I would like to live a long life," he said. "But I'm not concerned with that now. I just want to do God's will." God's will is to bring about the beloved community.

It also came as a shock to me that King was unpopular in his own time. In 1966, his approval rating stood at 32%, according to Gallup. A lover of justice in all its forms, King gave a speech denouncing the war in Vietnam that got him disinvited from an engagement at the White House. These are facts not exactly trumpeted on MLK Jr. Day.

After high school, I attended an only slightly less white elite private college. My junior year, I studied abroad at Oxford, where I had the novel experience of being an ethnic minority within my peer group. I formed a tight circle of friends with six other study-abroad students, and of those six, three were first generation Indian-Americans. There was also Nida, who was Muslim and from Mumbai. I had a crush on one of the guys, Sushil, whose family was from the Indian state of Kerala, which has a large Christian minority. Sushil was smart and funny; he was also incredibly dutiful and strait-laced, which was part of his charm. He and his family were all devout Christians. When I made my advances, it soon became clear that, as an atheist white girl, I was not going to make it with this pious Indian guy. Of course, it's possible I made up this explanation to soften the rejection, but, accurate or not, it was the one and only time in my life I ever perceived my race as a disadvantage.

I'm a fan of a well-placed expletive. My favorite sign at the rally, held by a white woman, read, "Fuck White Supremacy."

My Mental Troubles

June 2020

I have the less severe form of manic-depression known as Bipolar II, which means that I don't experience full-blown mania (not sleeping for days, thinking I'm God, spending exorbitantly), but I do go through periods of mild elation that can be followed by devastating lows. And for many people with mental troubles, COVID has made coping more difficult. Here's how my psychiatrist put it: "People with depression are struggling even more, people with anxiety are even more anxious, and people with substance abuse disorders are dealing with more frequent and intense cravings. Whatever your issue is, it's worse. This is a stressful time."

I joke that I got the mental illness with an upside. Most of the time, I move between my usual energetic self and periods of heightened focus, productivity, and expansiveness, in which I struggle to get enough sleep because my brain is overbrimming with ideas and things I want to do. I'm sensitive to the shifting seasons, and spring and summer tend to send me into overdrive. June sometimes finds me up at 5:00 AM gardening, at 4:00 AM composing emails to the Department of Public Works about a much-needed crosswalk, or at 3:00 AM getting my busy thoughts down in my journal. Basically, I run hot, sometimes too hot, and then I crash, hard—to the point where I wonder if I want to live at all.

But I'm lucky to be married to a man whose equanimity is of epic proportion. And thanks to a stint in McLean psychiatric hospital a few years ago, I now have a proven list of coping skills, one of which is congratulating myself for any small accomplishment, for instance, showering. And I'm learning to accept and feel curious about this vulnerability in my psyche rather than pushing it away with my eyes shut tight, ashamed, hoping it would just go away. Bipolar depression has a strong genetic component, more so than unipolar depression, and the research shows that although one can effectively manage the disorder, it *doesn't* go away. I've been dealt a slew of good cards in my life; I just happened to get this one shitty one.

June 2020

When I recovered from the depression that sent me to McLean, I wrote a letter to my future depressed self in which I tried to be sympathetic but also firm that those feelings of deadened hopelessness—that overwhelming sense of life's meaninglessness—however intense, would be transitory. Just acknowledging that I would almost certainly return to that dark place was difficult but, as it turned out, also freeing.

My depressive episodes come on suddenly (usually when something else is out of balance in my life), but mercifully, they don't last long, usually two to three months, and then I'll have long stretches—sometimes years—of being well. But since COVID began, I've been shuttling rapidly between elation and an anxiety-ridden blankness. One week the world is my oyster; the next, I'm a shell of a person. Last week, paralyzed, unable to make even the most banal decisions, I called my best friend, V., who ordered me to bike to her house and then instructed me to sit six feet away while she pulled weeds from a garden bed she was renovating. V. reminded me that I'd felt the same way a few weeks ago and it had passed: this was likely just another bad week, not the start of a mental breakdown. Cheerfully pulling up a clump of ferns, V. prescribed rereading a Jane Austen novel. My psychiatrist prescribed an increase in my mood stabilizer, "just for the time being."

Shame at taking a psychotropic medication was another thing I had to get over. Before COVID yanked my job away, I taught yoga to women recovering from drug addiction. I used to ask myself, "What kind of a phony yoga teacher takes psych meds?" Answer: A yoga teacher who can empathize with human suffering.

I'll Have the Unusual

June 2020

I could weep: I am so grateful the libraries are lending again. The drought of new reading material saw Rory and I rereading the same picture book six times a day. Though I'd occasionally catch a new detail in the illustrations or feel a fresh appreciation for a piece of phrasing, it was rather mind-numbing to turn to the same stack of stories over and over and over again. We've read *Madeline* so many times, Rory can, with minimal prompting, recite the story himself.

"On her bed ..."

"There was a crank!"

"And a crack on the ceiling ..."

"Had the habit of sometimes looking like a rabbit!"

His excitement never seems to wane. Mine does.

Pre-COVID, Rory and I visited the library weekly, checking out around twenty picture books. The bad ones were promptly returned, but the good ones were held onto for repeated savoring. When that circulation stopped and we were left with what we had (and some of it quite tedious), I was gripped with dread. The schools *and* the libraries closed? How will I survive?

When I told Rory we could get books from the library again, he requested we check out *The Boring People*. Puzzled, I asked him to describe the story, and realized he meant *Meet the Dullards* by Sara Pennypacker, illustrated by Daniel Salmieri. *Meet the Dullards* tells the story of a suburban couple mutually devoted to living as boring an existence as possible. When the Dullards take their three children out for ice cream, they all order vanilla cones: "Hold the cones. And extract the vanilla." The illustration shows the family, all dressed in grey, taking no pleasure in eating bland ice cream out of their cupped palms.

But then Mr. and Mrs. Dullard catch their children reading books about the circus and fear the neighborhood has had a corrupting influence. Mr. Dullard recalls the distress of seeing the leaves change color the previous fall. "And now this!" he cries, pointing out the window "to an upsetting commotion in the driveway." The illustration shows a giant suburban driveway in the foreground (with a row of identical houses in the background) where a lone snail makes its way across the asphalt. Wanting to make sure Rory got the joke, we paused to talk about how snails move and what "commotion" means. The next line is spoken by Mrs. Dullard. "Yes," she says, "this is no place to raise Blanda, Borely, and Little Dud."

By the time I'd hit Borely, I was laughing so hard I couldn't speak Little Dud aloud. It took me two do-overs to reach the end of the sentence. Rory was laughing too, but clearly as much at his mother's violent guffawing as the book itself.

The Dullards pack up and move to an identical suburb. The story ends with the children running off to join the circus. It's a black comedy, a cartoon of joyless suburban living, a scathing indictment of white flight. It's not that I'd suddenly discovered children's literature had value, but would I have laughed so hard, or pondered it so long, had it been one of the twenty books we'd checked out that week, like the week before, and the week before that?

On Beauty

June 2020

F ew things make me feel more alive than walking at dawn. Yesterday I woke at 4:40, the sky already brightening. I walked down to Quissett Harbor and then out along the Knob, a small spit of conservation land that ends in an ascent up stone steps to panoramic ocean views. As I walked the Knob's rocky southern shoreline, I could see there were two sets of clouds: a low, fast-moving stratum and huge, immobile cumulus clouds. The low bank in the east obscured the rising sun from the viewer on the ground, but the cumulus clouds were vantaged high enough in the west to catch the sunrise unobstructed, and as they did, their tops were lit a majestic purple-pink. I was full of the beauty of it as I headed west toward the Knob's pinnacle.

When I arrived, two young men were coming down the steps. They walked unsteadily, one of them holding a Gatorade bottle, and were clearly awake at dawn because they'd been up all night boozing.

"Beautiful morning," I said with enthusiasm.

The first man looked at me—sullen, incredulous—and the second said, "Wish I could see the sun."

"But the clouds are beautiful," I said, guessing they'd been staring east and hadn't turned around to see the towering pink clouds in the west, which by now had lost their glory.

At the top of the Knob, a family was clustered facing east. I tried my greeting again: "Beautiful morning."

"Too bad the clouds are in the way," the dad replied.

Stepping up on the rocks to face out over Buzzards Bay, I turned back with a sudden thought to share: "You know, clear sunrises are all the same; every cloudy sunrise is cloudy in its own way."

The mother smiled. She then remarked on the surface of the ocean, how beautiful it was this windless morning.

I departed down to the northern beach, its lone inhabitant. Endlessly interesting are the faces of the ocean.

That morning it was a strangely vibrant gray, a kind of charcoal-aqua. Without waves, and without direct light reflecting off its surface, I could see deep beneath the calm water: the light, open swathes of sand, the dark rocky patches. I didn't have my bathing suit on, and it wasn't a warm morning, but standing there at the edge of the sea, I felt certain that if I didn't get *in* that water, I would regret it the rest of my life. Was it the pandemic that so filled me with the urge? The resolve not to regret? I stripped and swam far from shore.

On Poetry and Prayer

July 2020

It's certain people are praying more these days. Praying not to get sick, praying their businesses will survive, praying for a vaccine. As a humanist, prayer doesn't come naturally to me.

The poet Mary Oliver loved to rise early and take a walk. Oliver described the dawn sky reflected in coastal ponds as prayers heard and answered "whether or not you have ever dared to pray." Every morning was Genesis to her—"every morning the world is created"—but she didn't care to get too particular about what she did and did not believe. In the fancifully skeptical poem "Angels," she writes, "I have lots of edges called Perhaps / and almost nothing you can call / Certainty."

Religious feeling electrified Emily Dickinson, but she was no Christian. Three years after the publication of *On the Origin of Species*, Dickinson wrote a poem that begins, "This world is not conclusion. / A species stands beyond — " It ends:

> *Much Gesture, from the Pulpit —*
> *Strong Hallelujahs roll —*
> *Narcotics cannot still the Tooth*
> *That nibbles at the soul —*

Religion (at least the organized kind) is an opiate— that fails to do the job. Yet Dickinson asserts *something* called the soul. What does she mean by "a species stands beyond"? Is she calling God a species beyond? Is she acknowledging that a force other than God created, and will continue to create, species? This much is clear: Dickinson's consciousness was extraordinary, and she found nothing holier.

> *The Brain — is wider than the Sky —*
> *For — put them side by side —*
> *The one the other will contain*
> *With ease — and You — beside —*

The Brain is deeper than the sea —
For — hold them — Blue to Blue —
The one the other will absorb —
As Sponges — Buckets — do —

The Brain is just the weight of God —
For — Heft them — Pound for Pound —
And they will differ — if they do —
As Syllable from Sound —

Henry David Thoreau, a disaffected Unitarian who famously resolved to live deeply, wrote to a friend, "I feel that I draw nearest to the great secret of my life in my closest intercourse with nature. There is a reality and health in (present) nature, which is not to be found in any religion … I suppose that what in other men is religion is in me love of nature." (Thoreau read the new account of our species' origin in 1860, six years after the publication of *Walden* and two years before his death at the age of forty-four.)

I consider myself both a Unitarian and a humanist; that you can be both is what allowed me to sign up for the former. I enjoy the fellow feeling of a community dedicated to social justice and self-reflection, a congregation that decided its members could use whichever bathroom they felt they belonged in, a place where people are passionate about saving the dwindling number of species left on this beautiful but troubled planet. I enjoy our minister David's wide-ranging preaching: his recounting of an all-night Voodoo ceremony he attended in a Boston suburb; the theological discussion he got into with a homeless man in New York City; and his reflections on growing up gay in West Virginia as one of Jehovah's Witnesses, a religion he had to lose to accept his sexuality. I enjoy the open-mindedness of a religion as liberal as Unitarianism, so liberal that, as my childhood girlfriend put it, "You can worship your toaster, and as long as you're not hurting anyone, they're cool with that." (Some count this as a defect.) But I find it difficult to *feel* the "spirit of life" when I sing about it indoors on Sundays under those energy-efficient LEDs that are always on no matter how much natural light is streaming into a sanctuary that, frankly, feels more like a corporate meeting room than a place of worship. We're a very brainy bunch; aesthetics and subjective experience get short shrift. I cringed the whole way through when, a few years ago, in celebration of National Poetry Month (April), a woman got up and read a florid piece of prose about the wonders of poetry that she'd found on the internet. My neighbor, a poet and a Quaker, told me this joke about the Unitarians: we're lined up at the gates of heaven; a sign pointing one way reads "God," and a sign pointing the other way reads "Discussions about God."

I know the terror of not being able to breathe. My childhood asthma sent me to the emergency room nearly every fall with that year's respiratory virus. I've watched my father's unconscious body agonize for a few futile minutes after the breathing tube was removed. People are dying horrible deaths from this virus. But I'm more concerned with coming to die and discovering I had not lived. And so there I stood, waist-deep in the ocean, my arms out from my sides, palms to the horizon, the tips of my fingers in the sea, and I prayed—"As long as I live, may I be ever alive to the beauty of this world"—then dove, and swam as far as I could before surfacing.

Remotely Learning

July 2020

When COVID hit, I was in the middle of taking a course on classical Indian philosophy and litera-ture through Harvard's night school. Students had the option of watching the lecture online, but I attended in person because I valued being in the room with the professor, Parimal, and also in the hallway with him after class; it's how we got to know each other. Parimal likes to move around while he teaches, and I enjoyed watch-ing him stride about the classroom, leaving the lectern to travel back and forth across the projector screen, as if the material were too exciting to teach at a standstill. When he'd ask a question designed to challenge us—to make us think twice about a potential but facile interpretation he'd just offered—he'd stop, tilt his head to the side, narrow his eyes, and then turn his chin slightly upward with an expression that said, "Let's think harder about this."

I would spend the night in Boston with friends, get up and write in a coffee shop, and then wander around the South Asian collection at the MFA before catching the bus home. This was eight months into my decision to get a self-directed graduate degree—a "PhD in becoming a better writer"—after being the primary parent to our two boys for most of the past twelve years. Then COVID struck, and that rich, interpersonal, three-dimensional world vanished. The course continued online from Parimal's home office, but he was now pinned in his seat, and the video often froze. After the first Zoom class ended, I shut the lid of my laptop and burst into tears.

My high school English teacher's mentor gave her a piece of advice that she's made a mantra of her professional life: "relationship over task." You have to know your students—be in tune with them emotionally, sense their interests and struggles—to guide them effectively. Online learning is 90% task. And being sensitive to your students' internal worlds is nearly impossible when they're white names on a black screen. My teacher, with whom I'm now friends, agrees online education is a shadow of the real thing, but she's worried about the increased risk returning to the classroom entails; children seem to handle this virus well, but my teacher is sixty-two, and I'm likewise concerned for her well-being.

I can accept it if schools don't open their doors in the fall, leaving my twelve-year-old to spend hours on the couch with his Chromebook rather than in the classroom with his peers—if that's what the greater good calls for, so be it—but I really scorn happy-face talk about online learning. Remote learning? More like "remotely learning." And for young children, it's even more of a joke. Virtual kindergarten? Please, spare me the charade.

Given our family's dynamics, my preference for Rory's education would be in-person kindergarten three days a week. This spring's stay-at-home order was a dream come true for my preschool-averse little boy. Rory doesn't like a lot of noise or commotion, and, though not exactly shy, he, as his teacher put it, "is not a social butterfly." Earlier this month, when we tried to send him to socially-distanced summer camp two days a week so he could practice being around other children again (and I could get a break from six months of stay-at-home-advisory mothering), he braced himself against the car door and then ran into the woods, screaming he was scared of coronavirus. If schools do reopen fully, it will be a shock to Rory's sensitive system. To go from zero to sixty, from home all day, every day with Mom to five days a week in a building teeming with children? Insisting on it will be emotionally painful for both of us, even if a vaccine miraculously appears overnight.

No Screen Time
without Clean Time

July 2020

It used to be that I did a fair amount of housework while the kids were at school, but when COVID closed the schools and my mother withdrew her babysitting, I was suddenly faced with a fraction of the time to do what I really wanted: study, read, and write. All of these require a long period of silence, a luxury I'm only afforded during the morning hours before the boys wake up and during the two hours every afternoon I allow them to play video games. Early on in COVID, I developed a motto for these special windows of time: thou shalt not do housework.

But the house still needs to be cleaned, the food cooked, and the laundry folded. So I've been training our boys to help around the house.

We now have a routine where the half hour before screen time is clean time. The boys did a fair amount of grumbling at first, which was met with impassioned variations on the following speech: "By refusing to help, you're watching my education, professional ambitions, and happiness go down the drain. Is it really fair that I waste my life in domestic servitude while you play video games? Get your twelve-year-old butt in the bathroom and clean the toilet."

It took me a while to learn which tasks Kunio, the twelve-year-old, did well. When he was asked to pick up the living room, I observed him absent-mindedly moving things from the living room floor to the kitchen counter; putting things where they belong is not his forte. But he's good at washing windows, shucking corn, scrubbing pots and pans, taking out the trash, and cleaning toilets. Kunio can now be relied on for substantial help around the house.

Little Rory is less reliable. Some days he digs in his heels and refuses to lift a finger. Cajoling, as well as lectures about fairness aimed at his prefrontal cortex, is ineffective. I could resort to punishment, but taking away his screen time would be self-defeating. So instead, I deploy lavish praise for any small effort. When he picks up his puzzle, I pick him up, kiss him, and tell him it makes my heart sing when he cleans up.

The other day he refused to pick up his toys, and I said, "Fine, but there's no video games until the living room is clean. So you can either help and play sooner, or sit and watch while your poor mother does all the work." After twenty minutes of peevish non-participation, he offered to do the vacuuming. Rory's a very thorough vacuumer. I think he enjoys being in charge of that big machine, knowing which button turns it on and which zips the cord up faster than a frightened snake.

Occasionally, I'll forget about clean time, and as I'm eagerly trotting off to get Rory the iPad, he'll remind me by saying, "And what's my chore?" Last week I was loading the dishwasher when he came over, picked a granola bar wrapper up off the floor, dropped it in the trash, looked up at me, and asked, "Mommy, does that make your heart sing?"

Masks Up!

August 2020

Early the other morning, I was walking south down Racing Beach Avenue, which is straight as an arrow, and far ahead a woman was walking north. I crossed to the opposite side of the street and pulled my mask up; she likewise raised hers from under her chin. It felt a bit like we were adversaries in a jousting contest, suiting up for the charge. Consequently, as we passed, I looked at her and smiled, hoping she'd see the friendliness in my eyes.

Mask etiquette is an incredibly complex addition to how we comport ourselves in public, and it makes me realize how rich, subtle and complicated even the most glancing interactions with strangers can be. I hope dozens of sociologists are studying this.

In Japan, where my father-in-law lives, mask-wearing is already normalized. Even absent a pandemic, a quarter of commuters on the Tokyo subway will be wearing masks, either for protection or because they have a cold. Cleanliness and a sense of duty towards the common good feature strongly in Japanese culture, and so it's unlikely many there feel awkward about what has been an enormous shift for us here in America. We're like self-conscious teenagers navigating a daunting new social behavior.

My friend, a nurse, observed that men seem to be mask-less more than women, and told me about a cartoon that lampooned the habit of wearing your mask over your mouth but not your nose, showing a man with his bathing suit drawn only to the top of his thighs. We devised another cartoon: a man with a condom tied in a bow around his erect penis.

Lacking empirical data on whether mask-wearing is correlated with gender, I can say, in defense of men, that I see plenty of women not wearing masks when they probably should be. The other day, I had mine in my lap, but I simply forgot to put it on when I pulled up to the Dunkin' Donuts drive-through window. Leaving your mask in your lap is even worse than neglecting to pull it over your nose.

Last week I was in line at the Woods Hole Market, where the woman cashier had her mask well below her nose—so much so that she was able to lick her finger to aid herself in picking up a pesky dollar bill when making change for the customer in front of me. I cringed, and when it came my time to pay, it was all I could do to force myself to move towards her uncleanly aura. Later I marveled at my revulsion to a behavior I wouldn't have batted an eye at six months ago.

It reminded me of the first time I'd gone to the grocery store after the stay-at-home advisory came down; I'd had the darndest time getting those flimsy produce bags open without using a little spit. Now I bring a damp cloth in my pocket so I can wet my fingers and separate the two sides and not have to stand there helplessly, like a child, pawing at the plastic.

Can't You Count Them?

August 2020

M y son Rory was in love with writing his letters when COVID closed his preschool in March. It's been sad to see his enthusiasm wane as the months have dragged on.

While I was making dinner a week after the state went into lockdown, Rory requested I spell different words on pieces of scrap paper, which he then copied onto our kitchen chalkboard in tidy little columns. After dinner, I looked at what he'd written. The central column read, "explosive / boom God / God / boom / boat / in boat / Mother Earth." It struck me as such a profound statement on the human condition that I, in turn, copied it into my journal. What's it all about? "Well, there was this explosion. Boom.

Creation. God. Boat. We're in a boat. The boat is Mother Earth." Through April, Rory continued to hunt up printed words around the house, copying them out into little books he'd construct by stapling several pieces of paper together. By the end of May, however, he'd forsaken his post as family scribe. I haven't seen him write anything in weeks.

Numbers, however, have newly captured his imagination. When we were riding our tandem bike back from Woods Hole the other day, Rory requested we count to one hundred, which we did, twice. But if I try to play teacher and sit him down for a writing or math lesson, he balks. After a painful week of trying to follow his preschool's suggestions for academic enrichment at home, I gave up. The agenda was annoying him and making me feel inadequate.

The other day, while swimming in Oyster Pond, Rory invented a game where he'd plunge his face into the water with his eyes open, and my job was to hold up a certain number of fingers below him. He'd then come up spluttering and report on how many digits I'd flashed him. When I used only one of my hands, he played the game with perfect accuracy. But after a dozen rounds, I got bored and threw him a curve ball, holding out my closed fist. He came up beaming. "Zero!" Another dunk. I held out both my hands, every finger splayed. He bobbed up, stumped. Kicking his legs harder to make up for the lost propulsion of his arms, he held his fingers in front of his face and counted them by nodding his head at each one, skipping one accidentally. "Nine," he declared.

"No. Ten. You have ten fingers."

Pause. I threw him another curve ball. "And how many toes do you have?"

He rolled his eyes and said wearily, "Can't you count them?"

"You have the same number of toes as you do fingers," I hinted. He wasn't interested in deducing anything.

Falmouth Schools have announced that students in grades K-6 have the option of either attending school full-time in person or full-time remote learning. A few of my friends have opted for the school's remote learning program, and others have chosen to independently homeschool their young children. I know Rory would prefer staying home with me, and it's indisputable that keeping him out of the public schools will reduce his chances of catching COVID, but I'm desperate to get back to my own reading and writing. Come September, I'll need to swallow the hard fact that what's best for my child and what's best for me don't align.

On Routines

August 2020

When COVID cracked apart daily life, my high school English teacher and I started a "poet of the month" club as a source of companionship and structure. We pick a poet, she sends me a list of poems to study, I choose a handful to memorize, and then we get together over Zoom to recite and analyze them. Though I majored in English, poetry is a region of literature I've been largely deaf to, until now. And I'm all the more astounded by this vast world of beauty, precision, and pleasure for having entered it so late. It was here all the time? Just waiting for me?

My late-coming to the land of poetry was due to a combination of laziness and ignorance. Poems were difficult; novels were more fun. And I didn't understand that silently reading poems doesn't get you very far. Speaking poetry is how it comes alive. And I need to speak poems many, many times over before I can meaningfully inhabit them either cognitively or emotionally.

I take the poems I'm memorizing copied out on index cards on my morning walks to the Knob at Quissett Harbor. Most mornings I pass an older gentleman on his way to or from his daily swim. He sees me and exclaims, "The poet!"

I bow and say, "Good morrow to you, sir."

He says, "And what is inspiring you today?" And I recite him a Shakespeare sonnet, or one of Emily Dickinson's dark yet whimsical ditties. He's a businessman with an old-money air and several yachts in the harbor, and he's keen on poetry. After listening, he'll always make an astute, appreciative remark. When I asked him once how he'd developed such a good ear, he told me his Andover prep-school education included memorizing poetry. We went on to lament the trend in secondary education towards reading non-fiction for information rather than literature for one's soul.

Most mornings I also see a woman out jogging on Quissett Harbor Road. The other day she was entering the trailhead to the conservation plot adjacent to our house just as I was exiting, and my presence startled her. I stepped aside to let her pass, catching her gaze and hoping she'd stop and we could learn each other's names. She continued down the trail and I felt sad at the missed connection. But then she stopped and turned round to face me: she'd just been getting far enough away to take down her mask.

"I've never seen anyone in these woods," she remarked.

"I live next to them," I said. "The Oyster Pond Environmental Trust bought the land a few years ago."

"I used to jog on the bike path. But it's so crowded now, and it's hard to jog with a mask on, so I ducked in here one day. These trails are wonderful."

"That's one upside to COVID," I said, "It pushes you out of your routines."

Life would be intolerable without routines, but they can also imprison, and they necessarily exclude alternatives. When this pandemic is over, I wonder how many of us will turn back, and in what way—gratefully or with reluctance, intentionally or mindlessly—to former modes of living. But I'm more curious about those who will have discovered new possibilities for seeing or being in the world and might turn away from lives over-full of stale routines and quiet desperation.

Turns in the Weather

September 2020

Yesterday I took my usual morning walk to Quissett Harbor, but the weather felt different: cool, windy, with a smell of autumn in the dry air. When I reached the Knob's pinnacle, I stepped atop the stone border of the summit's gathering platform and crouched down. The sun had just risen and was casting long shadows westward. My gaze came to rest on an enormous boulder offshore, one of those giant rocks swept along like pebbles by the glacier that plowed up the ridged spine of the Upper Cape and then plunked down as the ice melted amidst massive climate change. I could see the straight shadow of the pinnacle's stone border projected on the boulder's face. Then I noticed a little blob atop the straight shadow. Was it me? I sprang up and held my arms aloft. My shadow jumped up too. The wind was blowing hard out of the northwest, and the fabric of my thin, loose-hanging cotton pants fluttered as if panicked, like when a jib, the lines loosed, baffles wildly. I stood there, poised against the gale, watching my pants ripple on the rock below.

On my way back up from the harbor, I passed an older woman I used to see often back when I worked the front desk at the Woods Hole Library. We stopped to chat. Despite living alone, she was managing the pandemic well, she said, "but I'm nervous for the winter." Many of us are nervous about the winter. Our family has coped well with COVID, but I wonder how much of that has been thanks to the buoyancy of spring and the many pleasures of summer on the Cape. The approaching fall brings a sense of unease. Those of us who have been home with our children for the past six months are facing a winter with bleakly reduced options for keeping them occupied and playing with friends in the safety of the open air.

But then I think back to when COVID closed the schools and likewise suspended my job teaching yoga to women recovering from drug addiction; the prospect of being home with my squabbling children all day, every day, for weeks on end had terrified me. I'd joked with friends, "If this virus doesn't get me, I'll just kill myself." Then those weeks turned to months, and somehow I adapted.

At times I'll slip into that particular kind of self-flagellation that masquerades as gratitude. Many are suffering tremendous hardship through this pandemic, and their suffering makes my own anxieties about spending the winter in a warm house with plenty of food, my stably employed husband, and our just-fine-to-not-be-at-school boys seem like trivial sniffling. I must be a very pampered human being, a voice chides.

As I walked back to the house after sharing these reflections with my friend from the library, I saw the first crabapple of the season lying on the side of the road. I picked it up and walked on, tossing it lightly in the air. There was something reassuring about catching that small fruit in my hand over and over. Fall's coming, then winter. But spring will follow.

Remoter Parenting

September 2020

Schools open next week. When they closed in March, I was struck by an unexpected upside: I no longer had to get my children out the door so they could be somewhere on time.

My husband and I have a traditional division of labor; he's the breadwinner and I'm the primary parent. It's my job to get the kids to and from school, and when schools closed, I realized just how big a job it was. Released from this duty, I felt tremendous psychic ease, which was fortunate, as the pandemic brought a lot of just the opposite.

Kunio, our older boy, is nasty when awoken before 9:00. But as soon as his adolescent body was allowed to follow its own rhythm—stay up past midnight, sleep until 11:00—being around him in the morning was actually pleasant. As dismal as his spring-term Chromebook education had been, it did have the advantage of commencing only slightly before noon. And for Rory, COVID came in like a knight in shining armor to halt his tortuous education. Getting him to preschool had frequently been gut-wrenching. After prying him off me and running for the door, I'd sometimes just sit in my car and cry. Several months into the pandemic, I asked him if he missed school. "No," he said, "I only miss gymnastics."

Without the usual lineup of camps, Kunio spent much of the summer learning how to replace cracked screens on used iPhones and reselling them on eBay for a $20 profit. A few weeks ago, he managed to assemble a desktop gaming computer out of hand-me-down parts from his father and uncle. Now he can play *Titanfall 2* for hours rather than stopping after thirty minutes when his dad's puny old laptop overheats.

COVID has taught me this: kids can handle a surprising amount of neglect. In an age of hyperattentive parenting, this was a liberating discovery. We've always kept a strict screen time diet in our house, but with COVID, I quickly realized my mental health required throwing several of my parenting standards out the window. Rory now plays on the iPad every day for two straight hours while I do yoga, meditate, and then read or write for the remaining hour. The video games he plays are so stimulating (read: addictive) that he'll pee on the couch if I don't carry him to the toilet mid-way. He's also redeveloped his nervous habit of chewing on his shirt collar, so if I don't remove his shirt beforehand, he chews holes straight through the fabric. I'm not expecting a parenting medal.

When I'm not plugging Rory into mind-numbing entertainment, or feeding him, I largely ignore him. While I fold laundry, prep dinner, and read snatches of my novel, he looks at his comic books, gallops around the yard pretending he's playing Minecraft, and occasionally helps me in the kitchen. Most days this summer, the sum total of our quality time consisted of a morning board game and tickle session ("Stop, stop! Okay, do it again!"), swimming in the afternoon, and a snuggle and books at bedtime. Yet he seems content.

Next summer, if COVID is over, we'll send Kunio back to his sleepaway camp (no electronics allowed), but I won't clog his school-free months with lots of activities. And I won't send Rory to day camps; I'll just let him hang around the house, mostly ignoring him until we go to the beach in the afternoon, both of us happy he doesn't have to be anywhere at 9:00 in the morning.

Dreaming during a Pandemic

September 2020

I woke from the dream with tension all over my body. My husband had invited a small group of colleagues over for an outdoor lunch, but more and more of them kept showing up, all mask-less. Soon, a rowdy pack of scientists was jammed into our front lawn. Then these unwanted guests began wandering through the house. A woman came inside and asked for a cup of tea, then sneezed: I watched as a sooty black vapor came out her nose and dissipated in the air.

I ran down to the basement, where our two boys were playing video games, and rushed them into the car. (My husband had lost all control over the crowd and was trapped in its center.) The younger boy had trouble buckling his seat belt. I climbed into the backseat to help him, not realizing that I had already put the car in gear. It began rolling backward down our steep driveway. I lunged forward trying to press the brake pedal with my hand, but it was hopelessly out of reach. "Pull the emergency brake!" I shouted to my older boy in the front seat. The brake was hard for him to lift. The car kept rolling backward. He finally managed to lift it and I climbed into the driver seat and raced the car up our street.

I'm a vivid dreamer, and this was just the most recent of a string of bizarre nightmares about COVID. Just after the virus hit, I dreamt that a friend, who's a doctor and colonel in the United States army, was battling (with a sword) a paleolithic sea monster that was attacking from the sky.

A month ago, in real life, my older boy caught a puffer fish in Quissett Harbor. Then a week ago, I read a news article about the Vatican's request that—because COVID vaccines use stem cells from aborted fetuses—an alternative vaccine be developed for those with moral objections. The night after reading the article, I fell asleep and dreamt I was swimming in Quissett Harbor when a puffer fish with enormous teeth tried to attack me. With both hands, I grabbed the fish and held it at arm's length while it strained to bite my face. I succeeded in getting to shore safely, where I then entered a shipping container that was ludicrously perched on the yacht club's floating dinghy dock. Inside, coronavirus vaccines were being distributed. I requested the vaccine made with piranha blood.

You're Doing
the Right Thing

October 2020

Contrary to all my expectations, my son Rory's entry into socially-distanced kindergarten has gone remarkably well. Due to COVID, non-bus transport is being encouraged, and so for the first two weeks, I drove Rory to and from school. We'd park near the library and I'd haul his little bike out of the trunk so he could "bike to school" along the path that runs between Shivericks Pond and the school yard's back fence. To avoid crowding in the hallways, students enter the building at different times and through different entrances according to grade level. Kindergarteners meet in the back parking lot by the school garden and then proceed to their ground-floor classrooms, all of which have doors that open directly onto the lawn. The kindergarten teachers and a suite of additional staff are there to greet and organize the students. When Rory arrives on his bike, someone always says an excited hello, along with an "Oh my, you ride that bike very well, young man!"

The children then line up along yellow ropes hitched with knots every six feet. The students who arrived by bus are already waiting, holding the knots their name tags dangle from. The drop-off window for kindergarteners arriving by foot, bike and car is 9:15–9:30 AM. The cars pull up to the curb, and the staff, like cheerful valets, help the tiny children open their doors and climb down. "Good morning! Welcome! Do you need help getting that backpack on?" The teacher then picks up the front of the class rope and leads her line of masked and socially-distanced ducklings to the classroom.

As a mother who was terrified at the prospect of getting her preschool-averse, homebody little boy to a new school five days a week after six straight months home with mom, I'm beyond grateful to the school staff for making the management of a logistically complex start of the school day seem like a happy and wonderful task they are honored to perform—even in the rain.

At the start of his fourth day, Rory paused on his bike and said, "Mommy, I hate school."

My body tensed. Here we go again. But I tried to stay calm and sympathize. "Going to kindergarten is a big change for you."

He nodded and biked on but was then distressed to see his class already entering the building on the other side of the fence. "They've already gone in!" he cried, unwilling to go further. "It's too late. Let's go home."

"Mrs. LaCroix!" I called out to a teacher walking her children by. "Rory is worried he's late."

Mrs. LaCroix stopped and reassured Rory that his classmates had gone in a bit early and that people were waiting for him in the parking lot. "So just go down to where you always go. You're doing the right thing, Rory."

That day he came home full of pride at the purple plastic slinky he'd received for getting enough stickers on his behavior chart. "You get stickers when you follow directions and are nice to people. I got four stickers today!"

Last week Rory requested to try riding the bus to school. I called the director of transportation to get his bus pass and assigned seat number. Our house is at the top of a steep driveway halfway down a dead-end street, and I'd neglected to tell Rory that the bus stop is at our street's intersection with Woods Hole Road. I made him breakfast, a peanut butter sandwich and fried egg. He was sitting on the front porch.

"Rory, your breakfast is on the table."

"Can you bring it out to me?"

I humored him and put the plate beside him. "What are you doing out here?"

"I'm waiting for the bus."

Essential

October 2020

The other day my husband, an oceanographer, looked up from his iPhone and said, "I've been invited to a conference next summer."

"Where?" I asked, "Lala Land?"

When COVID first slammed us inside our houses, I read an article by a Harvard epidemiologist who predicted that periods of social distancing were likely to continue into 2022, our caution expanding and contracting in response to rising and falling infection rates. I'd felt dread, disbelief, and irrational rage at the researcher.

Now my pulse stays steady at the premonition that schools won't be open for long and that social distancing is here for the unforeseeable future. A friend whose daughter has started in-person kindergarten urged me to put aside my pessimism: "Our numbers are really good."

Fearing an imminent rise in infection rates, my hairdresser (I hadn't been in six months) has both her children home for online schooling: "We'll be lucky to make it to Thanksgiving." She knows a hairdresser in town who contracted COVID; other salons have gone under.

Last weekend, I drove out to camp in Western Mass. with my twelve-year-old son, his best friend, and the friend's mother—all in the same car, no masks. They're one of the few families we've continued to see through COVID, but always distanced and outside. This was our first time in close quarters. Our boys played cards in the back seat, and sharing the driving made the trip much easier. It was an acknowledged risk. Her son sneezed. Just allergies. But I still opened my window to let the swift highway air rush in.

Thursday afternoons, after we wash our hands for twenty seconds, I take my boys to their piano lessons at the conservatory, where we hear a men's a capella group practicing six feet apart in the courtyard.

What's essential? How much can we safely relax our guard? I squirm when I drive past restaurants' plate-glass

windows and see diners clustered together. Will the governor soon shoo us apart and back into our houses? Will
those restaurants survive?

I stood atop the Knob at Quissett Harbor on a recent,
misty morning. Through the vapor, the sun looked like
a shiny dime, its circumference crisp as the full moon's.
I watched as the fog traveled swiftly to the north. It was
dense, then thin, then thick again, with the sun dimming
and brightening. Then a long, thick stretch hid the sun entirely. I descended from the Knob's pinnacle and headed
back through the woodland towards the harbor. When I
emerged from the arched thicket of honeysuckle by the
yacht club, I looked up, and there was the sun again,
brighter than before.

The Procreant Urge

October 2020

Just before sunrise, I was standing atop the knobbed spit of conservation land that shelters Quissett Harbor when a young man appeared, carrying an old-fashioned picnic basket with a yellow rose laid atop its hinged wooden flaps. It's unusual to see anyone but the occasional fisherman out at that hour.

"A picnic?" I asked.

He looked up, fresh-faced, eager, a bit flustered, and said, "I'm actually about to propose."

"I'll leave."

"Sorry to interrupt."

"Please, not at all," I said, making a hasty exit. As I walked the rocky shoreline towards Racing Beach, I glanced back every so often, hoping the young woman (or man, or undeclared) had said yes.

It's heartening, when so much feels suspended and negated, to sense life flowing forward. Babies are being born, young men are proposing marriage, my niece just got her first job, the earth is still turning round the sun. It's wondrous to feel the awesome power of our homeostatic planet, its teeming blanket of biology a vital exception in a solar system otherwise composed of rocks, ice, dust and vapors—a place of unfathomable temperature extremes that make "boiling" and "freezing" seem like the tame cousins of our happy domesticity. Life, our being here at all, is a secular miracle, and it presses forward with an irrepressible force. As the capacious Walt Whitman, who scandalized nineteenth-century America with his sexually unrepressed poetry, put it: "Urge, and urge, and urge. Always the procreant urge of the world."

It was not without sympathy for those hormone-addled adolescents that I read about the recent house party in Woods Hole, where police reported that "not a single one" of the teens was wearing a face mask. For me, high school was a time of abundant physical affection. My girlfriends and I would sit on each other's laps and walk with our arms slung around each other; the guys would wrestle with each other at parties, perhaps hoping the girls would enjoy the display of strength; we'd all pile on couches and give each other piggy-backs. Touch, playfulness, sexual exploration: young adulthood is saturated with it. Even before COVID, I worried for the psyches of young people whose social lives are being increasingly subsumed by the digital.

Just after COVID struck, before masks were required in stores and social distancing was only loosely observed, I met a neighbor out walking. As a Neighborhood Falmouth volunteer, she was continuing to bring groceries to a woman in her nineties who lived alone. After delivering the groceries, my neighbor held back (more out of concern for the woman's vulnerable age than her own health) from ending the exchange with her customary hug. The woman insisted—virus be damned—that my neighbor still embrace her.

How do you withhold a hug from a woman who's almost one hundred—a hug she probably wants more than the groceries?

On Small-town Politics

November 2020

As I write this, I do not know who won Tuesday's Presidential Election. But I do know that I cherish small-town politics precisely because whether you're a Democrat or a Republican doesn't predetermine how you feel about local affairs, and you're unlikely to make nasty personal judgements about a neighbor who takes a different view of town politics.

Where the new senior center ought to be located is not an issue decided along party lines. Candidates don't run for the Select Board as Republicans or Democrats—thank God. School committee members with opposing national politics can work fruitfully together to craft a truancy policy. And townspeople are more likely to make up (or even change!) their minds based on a reasoned as-sessment of facts. Get us talking about national politics, though, and we tend to turn into belligerent sports fans.

I was in Shaw's this past Saturday afternoon, a mis-take I won't repeat. As someone who usually does her grocery shopping in the quiet hours after dinner, I was unprepared for the task of social distancing in a crowded grocery store. Relieved to be done at last, I headed for the check-out, but the lines were all full, with people standing dutifully on the six-foot-spaced red squares. Where to wait? I got behind a middle-aged woman and was relieved to see the man in front of her move off his red square and up to the conveyor belt. But then the woman in front of me didn't move up to the now vacated red square. I guessed it was because she felt the man had moved up prematurely, getting too close to the woman who was now paying for her groceries: she was going to play by the rules, even if no one else was.

Caught between crowding her and creating a road-block in the perpendicular aisle running from the bakery to the produce section, I maneuvered my cart sideways, which put me about three feet from the woman. She turned around with a cold look and said curtly, "Could you please move back?"

I felt like responding, "Well, how about you just move forward?" But I caught myself, and, making an effort to speak in a tone that sympathized with her discomfort but also communicated mine, I said, "I would, but I'm trying to let the people behind me get by." I was hoping she'd understand my plight and move up to the empty red square. The little white shoe prints looked so inviting. How could she resist?

But resist she did. Looking about, I realized I could push my cart to the opposite side of a wooden sale crate that stood to the woman's right, effecting a ninety degree turn in the line. Sincerely pleased, I exclaimed, "Ah, I'll move over here."

She visibly relaxed. "Thanks." A few moments later, she moved forward and I took her place in line.

The whole interaction played out over less than ten seconds, but I'd like to think that in that short period of time, she'd come to see the situation from my point of view. Her "thanks" wasn't a passive-aggressive "thanks for finally following the rules, you thoughtless space invader"—it was genuine appreciation.

I'm in love with the printed word, with the power of writing to transmit ideas, but there are drawbacks to the disembodied word. Amplifying toxic vitriol on Facebook, for instance, rarely leads to self-reflection or mutual understanding. And this is another virtue of local politics— its physicality. People literally come together for Town Meeting, where they stand and voice their opinions; selectman Doug Jones frequently jogs through our neighborhood; at the polls, people holding signs for opposing state senate candidates greet each other without enmity; acquaintances run into each other at the post office and ask with curiosity and an open mind, "Are you going to vote for the tax override?"

It's not that small-town politics always feels like a day at manners school. It can get ugly. And I've written some snide letters to the editor. But you're more likely to be held accountable when you're never more than three degrees from the person you've been unkind to.

Profit Margin

November 2020

COVID has been a wet dream for Amazon, an apoca-lyptic horseman for small businesses. As a writer, I worry most about the fates of Eight Cousins Bookstore and this paper.

Earlier this week, I interviewed the paper's editor and publisher, Bill Hough, about the company's finances. (Full disclosure: Bill was my boss when I worked as a *Falmouth Enterprise* reporter from 2013 to 2015, and I now consider him a friend.) Bill didn't feel comfortable going on record with a vividly worded description of how he'd felt when COVID hit and advertising revenue dropped 50%. "Let's just say it looked very grim," he said. A federal Paycheck Protection Program grant of $370,000 rescued the paper for this fiscal year, but the future remains uncertain.

The *Enterprise* has been independently owned since its establishment in 1895 and has been in the Hough family for three generations. Bill hopes his son John, who currently manages the advertising department, will take over when he retires. "I don't want to sell the paper to some awful corporation that's going to suck the life out of it."

The good news is that ad revenue has crept back up and is now down only 30%. Subscriptions are up, with a total of 11,000 print subscribers across the Upper Cape and 600 online subscribers. However, circulation accounts for only one-fifth of the paper's revenue, and the local businesses that are the paper's main source of income are bleeding cash.

People make fun of the *Enterprise*, its provinciality, calling it the *Emptyprise*. I get the joke. The paper is heavy on municipal minutiae, which, though essential for self-governance, doesn't make for scintillating reading. But you don't have to be a civic superstar to enjoy hearing about the waitress who got a $1,000 tip at C Salt Wine Bar

& Grill. And honestly, who doesn't love reading the police news? Only the people in it.

I am continually heartened by the robustness of Falmouth's civic life. And the *Enterprise* plays a critical role in this, not just through the information it provides (about ballot questions, vacancies on town committees, the school department's budget woes, etc.), but through fostering a sense of ourselves as a political and social community. It helps us care about this place. Scores of residents volunteer for Falmouth's nonprofits, and this paper prints their press releases for free, something AIM Media is unlikely to do.

Bill doesn't pay me to write this column. He can't afford to, not now. And because I'm doing this for free, it allows me to make the following exhortation with a certain amount of disinterest: please support the paper. If a friend doesn't subscribe, give her a subscription for the holidays. Tell business owners you saw their ad in the paper. If you're one of the lucky business owners benefitting from COVID, consider if advertising in these pages might boost revenue further.

And for the insanely wealthy among us—and I know you're here this off-season, on the run from city life in the time of COVID—please consider buying the paper and turning it into a nonprofit if the alternative is selling it to a corporation that only knows how to care for the bottom line.

And please, please support your town's sole remaining bookstore. Shipping isn't free, but your neighbor might work there. And writers need to make a living too.

COVID's Cairns

December 2020

When COVID hit, the cairns began appearing in force. These piled stone structures have been a part of human culture since prehistory, serving as burial markers, ceremonial objects, and aids to navigation. When you're hiking on a foggy mountain ridge, seeing a cairn come out of the mist means you're still on the path. And cairns have always been part of Falmouth's landscape, too, but never to this degree. The slender, balanced cairns that have proliferated on our shores since the start of the pandemic have no practical purpose and a less specified meaning. I read them as testimonials that a fellow human stopped here and—consciously or not—felt a desire to express being alive in this troubled world by balancing a few stones on top of each other. I feel a rush of kinship when I round the point on the southwest shore of the Knob to find the boulders there studded with dozens of these little totems. A few of my friends don't like the cairns, finding them an egotistical assertion of the builders' will in the midst of a natural scene. But I'm almost always happy to see them.

Cairns are folk sculptures. Anyone over the age of three can build one, and I sometimes try my hand at it. But not all of them are technologically simple. Some are testaments to an engineering genius of staggering proportion. They stand as skyscrapers amid their humble cottage brethren. There's a defiance in them, not just of gravity, but a defiance—as objects of beauty, integrity, endurance—of the hardship of this pandemic.

On a sunny, blustery afternoon, I was walking along the Trunk River section of the bike path when I came upon a magnificent cairn. I snapped a picture with my phone but was disappointed, on returning to the house and showing the photo to my husband, to find that the image conveyed nothing of the structure's awe-inspiring skill. I'd thoughtlessly framed the cairn from a standing-angle looking down, so that its outline was hardly distinguishable from the rocks that formed the background.

"I'll go back and try again."

The wind was gusting 25 mph, and my husband said, "It'll have blown over."

"Ye of little faith."

Not only had the cairn not blown over, but a dozen feet away stood another, even more spectacularly poised than the first.

On Death

December 2020

I was walking in Beebe Woods on a misty morning when I saw a friend from my Unitarian-Universalist fellowship, Lew Stern, coming towards me on the trail. Lew introduced me to his companion, Roger Kligler, who was moving slowly with the aid of two walking sticks. "Roger's leading the lawsuit to legalize physician-assisted death in Massachusetts," Lew said.

I'd read about the suit in the paper. It seeks the right for doctors to prescribe a lethal set of medications to terminally ill patients with less than six months to live. The cocktail induces a deep sleep and then gradually stops the lungs. Both a physician and a patient are plaintiffs in the case.

Tentatively, I asked Roger, "Are you the patient who's terminally ill?"

Roger stiffened. I could tell he didn't like the phrasing. "I have an incurable cancer," he replied. Then, looking straight at me, he said, "I am going to die."

I put my hand over my heart and exclaimed, "Me, too!"

Roger smiled.

Lew said, "Elizabeth's a writer."

"What's your specialty?" Roger asked.

"Perception."

"Of what?"

I swept my hand grandly before me. "Everything."

Roger wasn't sure how to take that. I broke out of the persona, and holding up my bundle of index cards explained, "I'm memorizing Walt Whitman's 'Song of Myself.' So I'm not feeling very modest."

Roger brightened. "Do you know my wife? Cathy Kligler? She's very perceptive, tries to lead an examined life."

"Good," I replied. "Because the unexamined one is not worth living."

It's the line that launched Western philosophy, what Socrates said at his trial when he refused to recant his behavior of questioning powerful Athenians as to the true nature of justice and virtue, thereby publicly exposing their poorly reasoned beliefs and leaving the prominent persons embarrassed. The jury found Socrates guilty of

impiety and corrupting the youth, and the prosecutor requested the death penalty. According to Athenian law, the
defendant then suggested his own sentence and the jury
chose between them. Socrates got up and first proposed
he receive free meals in the public square for the rest of
his life because he was the gods' gift to Athens, then suggested a modest fine. The jury sentenced him to death.

Socrates' friends then bribed the prison guards and
offered to smuggle him to a neighboring city state, beyond the reach of Athenian law. But Socrates declined;
however much he disagreed with the jury's verdict, he
preferred to obey the laws of his beloved city than weaken
them through evasion. With his distraught disciples as-
sembled around him, Socrates took the cup of hemlock
from the executioner, drank it, circumambulated the cell,
and lay calmly down to die.

I stepped towards Roger and recited the opening
lines of movement seven of "Song of Myself:"

> *Has anyone supposed it lucky to be born?*
> *I hasten to tell him or her it is just as lucky to die,*
>   *and I know it.*
> *I pass death with the dying, and birth with the*
>   *new wash'd babe, and am not contain'd*
>   *between my hat and boots.*

Americans worship optimism; we do a bad job at facing death. A friend of mine is an ER doc in Western Mass, and when COVID struck and the ER filled with already frail nursing-home patients, he intubated many of them with reluctance, feeling that he was doing more harm than good, that life support would merely prolong their suffering. My father always said to me, "Elizabeth, if it comes to that, I want you to pull the plug." Thankfully, I was able to do just that—legally—when he lay in an MGH hospital bed after a piece of plaque from his infected heart had broken loose, flown up his arteries, and blocked the blood to his now-dead brain.

Digital Christmas

December 2020

I grew up in Harvard, Massachusetts, where the Unitarian church sits atop the Harvard Common, a gently sloping triangle of parkland in the center of town where the original townspeople grazed their livestock. We weren't a devout family, even by Unitarian standards, but we did usually attend the Christmas Eve service, where the youth group acted out the nativity and the congregation then processed down the hill to gather around an enormous spruce strung with white lights at the base of the Common.

We each carried a small white candle with a paper doily, and once we were gathered around the tree, the minister would light one candle; the flame was then passed around, spreading exponentially, until we all held a flickering light emblematic of the divine light within. Despite being more than uncertain about the nature of divinity, the ritual always moved me.

Falmouth's Unitarian-Universalist Fellowship uses the same small white candles with the same paper doilies (which, a friend has informed me, is not that remarkable: nearly every church in America uses those candles). At the end of our Christmas Eve service, we turn off the lights and sing "Silent Night" as the flame of our common humanity is passed around. Then the lights come on and we burst into a jubilant "Go Tell it on the Mountain." I stand there next to my mother, joyful and triumphant, if not particularly faithful.

Singing together over Zoom is intolerable, and so it was with trepidation and below sea-level expectations that I dialed into our virtual Christmas Eve service this year (ten minutes late because I'd lost track of time while doing the dishes). The sermon was on the nineteenth-century Unitarian minister Edmund Sears, who was fired by his congregation for being too effeminate (read: queer) and who wrote the carol "It Came Upon a Midnight Clear." After a pre-recorded performance by the choir, our minister directed us to dim our house lights, light a candle, and switch from "speaker view" to "gallery view" so we could see as many of our fellow parishioners as possible. I tried to scroll through to see everyone's face in thumbnail, but seemed stuck on my current gallery. I hadn't even been thinking about looking for my mother when I caught sight of her in the bottom left corner of my screen, a candle lighting her face against the dark. She must have already been looking at me because, when I brightened with recognition, she beamed and waved, an almost girlish wave. Immediately I was crying.

Anti-Social Media

January 2021

Despite socially distanced seating, fall Town Meeting failed to reach a quorum. People felt caught between two opposing civic duties: voting and abstaining from large gatherings. And so Town Meeting will be held electronically this month. It's an appropriately extreme adaptation, but I worry we're opening Pandora's box.

Once a procedural system is in place for allowing people to stay at home, it may be tempting to use the electronic model when it is merely convenient. Snow storm? Let's convene in the ether. On vacation? That's okay, you can vote remote. I once heard a woman propose that Town Meetings be held electronically so that no one had to drive their cars to gather as a legislative body, making the evening carbon neutral. Making choices when our values are in conflict is difficult, but that suggestion works better as parody.

So much will be lost by not coming together physically. A great deal of civically significant networking and casual conversation occurs at an in-person Town Meeting that will be impossible to replicate over the internet. A sense of duty towards the common good is uniquely stirred when you're seated amid hundreds of your fellow citizens. You might even have a polite conversation with the person sitting next to you as to why he or she holds an opposing political position.

The digital utopists who delivered social media promised a more connected and friend-filled world. It's now clear the technology spreads more ill will than good. A naive froth over the democratization of self-expression obscured the drool over advertising revenue that actually drove social media on. And power over huge swaths of our political discourse is now in the hands of a few corporations.

Though self-selecting "social" media, we withdraw from actual dialogue in the public square. Driven by deep instincts of tribalism, we retreat into online spaces where everyone around us hates the same people. Like rats pressing the pleasure lever until they die of starvation, we're hooked on a digital discourse of one-line zingers that masquerades as political participation while it undermines critical thinking and civil society.

It's worse than Pandora's box: we compulsively open it again and again, and out fly ever more lies, intolerance, alienation, and rage.

On Zooming

January 2021

On January 19th of last year, Zoom stocks were trading at $75 a share. On October 19th, the price peaked at $568. We're all on Zoom, and anyone who invested early hit the jackpot.

As with Google, Zoom is now a verb—"Shall we zoom soon?"—and how to Zoom introduced a complex new set of social etiquette. Strong backlighting is a bad idea; an uncluttered background is a welcome courtesy. I periodically look at my camera so the other person can get the sense that I'm looking directly at them, even though I actually need to take my eyes off their face to do so. The inability to look each other in the eye is one of Zoom's most unsatisfying features. Another drawback is the distraction posed by your own image hovering there in the upper right. I'd Zoom a friend but then, like a modern-day Narcissus, spend half the time entranced by my own reflection.

So the discovery of the "hide self-view" option came as a relief; others can still see me, but I can't see myself. Last week, when I dialed into Sunday service with my Unitarian Fellowship, I chose to turn my camera off entirely so that my getting up and down to tend to my five-year-old, Rory, didn't distract other parishioners. Mid-way through the sermon, Rory brought me his new kaleidoscope and wanted me to look through it. I humored him, twirling the tube this way and that in front of my screen, watching the fractured image of our guest preacher, Saramaria Allenby, as she expounded the virtues of resilience and perseverance.

I then set the kaleidoscope beside my computer and fiddled with it for a few seconds before turning my attention back to the screen—where, instead of a black screen with my name in white letters, I saw a thumbnail video stream of myself. Unbeknownst to me (because I'd been looking through a kaleidoscope), Rory had turned my camera on. I blushed and dove for the Stop Video button. My fellow congregants must have wondered why I'd chosen to briefly display myself goofing off in the midst of the service.

Being together over Zoom is different: imagine sitting in a sanctuary, absorbed in a good sermon, when your neighbor pulls out a kaleidoscope, trains it on the minister, and gives it a few quizzical turns.

Mind Your Mask

February 2021

The other night, I dreamt I was at Shaw's. My shopping list was hard to read, unwanted items kept showing up in my cart, and when I finally got to the check-out, I realized I wasn't wearing a mask. It's the COVID equivalent of the public speaking nightmare—the one where you realize you're not wearing any pants.

A few days before this dream, I was in Shaw's in real life, heading towards the bakery, when an adolescent boy a dozen feet in front of me turned around, pulled down his mask, and shouted shopping instructions back towards his father.

"Put your mask up," I said sharply.

The boy hadn't been thinking—he'd just wanted to make sure his father heard him—but shouting projects saliva droplets, precisely what masks are meant to obstruct. My reaction had been swift, nearly automatic, and because he was a child, I hadn't worried about appearing to scold him.

I remember being in Shaw's the Friday schools were shut down. None of us were wearing masks. We were busy guarding ourselves against the virus by buying lots of toilet paper.

A few weeks ago, I opened the door to the Falmouth post office and saw a man bent over the center table, addressing a package—no mask. My body tensed, and I turned and went out the door, which hadn't yet closed behind me. It's possible the man had simply forgotten to put his mask on when he left the house. I could have tried a polite, "Excuse me, sir, but I think you may have forgotten to put your mask on." But that would have required getting closer to him, and my entire being was propelling me in the opposite direction. Plus, speaking up is difficult. A few months ago, I spent several minutes eyeing a man in the produce section of Shaw's who had his mask below his nose. Did he not know that masks need to also cover your nose to be effective? Did he simply not realize his mask had slipped down? I imagined the man sneezing.

What then? Would I regret not speaking up? I came close to informing him of the error but lost my nerve.

One morning last week, Rory's bus driver and I had a friendly chat while he mounted those giant steps and found his seat. I waved as the folding door shut and the bus trundled off. A moment later, I was struck with dread: Rory hadn't been wearing a mask. I called the school and made an agitated confession. "It's okay," the woman at the front office told me, "They have plenty of extras on the bus."

When Rory got off the bus that afternoon, the driver told me Rory had realized the mistake himself and gotten his spare mask out of his backpack. Rory confirmed the story, beaming at his self-sufficiency. There had been a line of cars stopped on Woods Hole Road when Rory had hopped barefaced onto the bus. Surely some of the drivers had noticed the public health violation? I would have been grateful had one of them rolled down their window and shouted, "Hey lady, put a mask on your kid!"

What's Wrong
with This Picture?

February 2021

I recently ordered Thai food from Bangkok Cuisine, which is closed to in-person dining but open for take-out. As I walked down Main Street, I passed another restaurant where it seemed that every other table was occupied; diners ate and talked barely six feet from strangers doing the same, all mask-less. I looked through the window as though these people were aliens inhabiting a different planet—or as though I were looking back in time, a happy flashback to before the pandemic.

Our neighbor is an anesthesiologist at a public hospital in Boston that filled to capacity last April. She volunteered for the COVID-19 vaccine trial and is considering signing her children up for the first phase of pediatric trails. Standing at the Woods Hole playground last weekend, watching our children fly kites with their masks on, she told me she is furious that restaurants are still open. Restaurant owners would no doubt feel furious—desperate—if the governor shut them down again.

Seventeen percent of people with COVID never show symptoms, according to a meta-analysis of thirteen studies that collectively tracked 21,708 subjects, published in November in the journal *Nature*. Asymptotic carriers of the virus are half as likely to infect others, but they're more likely to be out and about, socializing with friends in restaurants, for example. We all make choices to refrain or engage in officially permitted behaviors that nonetheless contribute to community spread. But my skin crawls to think of sitting near strangers in a small space without masks on; it would be one of the most unpleasant meals of my life. My mother's partner's best friend just died of COVID. He was seventy-seven, a widower, newly engaged.

On the Merits of
Gruesome Fairy Tales

February 2021

It's something only a librarian would know, and it surprised me when, four years ago, I began shelving books as the newest hire at the Woods Hole Library: the stories humans have been telling their children for centuries—folktales, fairy tales, legends—are shelved in non-fiction, call number 398.2.

Reading aloud a well-conceived picture book is one of parenthood's great joys. William Steig is a stylist beyond compare; the plain-spoken poetry of *Goodnight Moon* is eternally fresh; Arnold Lobel and Mo Willems' portrayals of friendship (between Frog & Toad and Piggie & Elephant, respectively) are as goofy as they are profound. The list goes on. But contemporary children's literature is of uneven value, and finding gems in the picture book section can require burrowing through heaps of newly-minted stories that are saccharine, boring, didactic, and frequently rendered in verse that rhymes but is otherwise atrocious.

Head over to the 398.2s, though, and you'll find a long parade of cultural home runs. In large libraries, this single hitch in the Dewey decimal system spans dozens of feet of shelf space. The human imagination has sifted and curated these stories over hundreds of years; they're richly structured, wickedly funny, tragic, delighting, and magnetic enough to have borne thousands of retellings. They also tend to be long, and so it's only recently that my five-year-old, Rory, acquired the requisite attentional stamina.

Traditional children's stories are instructional, told not just to entertain and pass the time, but as tools to help young minds meet a complicated world. While most do gesture towards goodness, insipid moralizing (à la Thomas the Tank Engine) is shunned, and badness doesn't get a sugar-coating. Centerstage are suffering, death, violence, and cruelty. Can you imagine a children's book today opening with a vicious queen telling her servant to cut out the bloody heart of her pubescent step-daughter for the crime of being beautiful? Or an impoverished father abandoning his children in the woods to starve, where they are captured by a woman intent on cannibalizing them? "Hansel and Gretel" is the original "Don't take candy from strangers" story. That old woman who lived in a shoe? The one with so many children she didn't know what to do? When the verse first appeared in print in the eighteenth century, "She gave them some broth without any bread; / whipped all their bums, and sent them to bed." Contemporary collections censor the verse: the woman beset with more children than she can feed now kisses them before tucking them in.

But alongside the old-school misery and deprivation stride cunning, triumph, and joy. Wish fulfillment abounds. And yet those happy endings are often a matter of luck ("happy" derives from the Old English "hap," meaning chance), and usually come at another's expense (Snow White's stepmother is so enraged at the girl's resurrection and royal wedding that she falls down dead); much is unresolvable; life is precarious. Especially during a pandemic, tidy dramas—where everyone's a winner—just taste like cheap, store-bought cake: Rory and I are reading exclusively out of the 398.2s.

Rory is particularly taken with "Jack and the Beanstalk." For weeks, he has been asking me and his father, "What if we were very poor and only had one cow?" Jack's story has gotten mixed up with an Armenian folk take, "One Fine Day," where a fox drinks an old woman's pail of milk and she retaliates by cutting off his tail. The woman promises to give his tail back if the fox gets her another pail of milk. But the cow withholds the milk and asks for grass, the grass asks for water, the maiden with the water jug asks for a blue bead, and the peddler with the beads demands grain. Then an old farmer takes pity on the fox and breaks the potentially endless quid-pro-quo by giving him some grain for free. The fox works backwards to satisfy everyone's desires and gets the milk and his tail sewn tenderly back on.

The other day I answered Rory that I would milk our only cow, drink what I needed to survive, and sell the rest at market. That really got him going: "What would you trade the milk for? Magic beans?" (Jack's mother beats him for doing such a stupid thing and throws the useless beans out the window.) "Would you trade it for a chicken? What if a man offered you wood for free to build a chicken house? And what if the chicken laid three eggs and one of them was gold?"

Last week, Rory woke up with sniffles and a cough, and I took him to get a COVID-19 test. The nurse who entered the exam room told him the giant q-tip about to be shoved up his nose was "just going to tickle." I played along.

"Do you want to sit in Mom's lap?" she asked.

Rory climbed up to sit sideways across my legs, dutifully lowered his mask, and tilted his head back. "Brave boy," I told him just before the nurse rammed the swab stick into his sinus cavity. He startled; I winced; stunned, betrayed, he burst into tears.

When he'd finished crying, he asked, "Can we go home now?"

"No. We have to wait for the test results."

"Can we read a book?"

Anticipating time in the waiting room, I'd thrown a few 398.2s into my bag. I pulled out "Princess Furball," an ingenious variant on the Cinderella story, one of hundreds of traditional riffs on the theme. The story opens with a neglected princess escaping from her palace home upon learning that her father has betrothed her to an ogre in exchange for fifty wagons of silver. I could feel Rory relaxing against me as we read of Princess Furball's crafty exploits as a kitchen slave and her eventual marriage to the young, handsome (and much better) king from the next kingdom over.

The doctor came in and announced Rory's test was negative. As I folded the results certificate into my bag, Rory asked, "What if there were only two shots in the whole world that made you not get coronavirus?"

"Two vaccine shots?" I clarified.

"Yes, two vaccine shots. And what if I got one and my

friend got the other? We could play together! Without our masks!"

The 398.2s mine and display our deepest fears and longing; they connect us to each other, to being human; and they've been at it so long they're considered cultural artifacts, complex moral visions inherited from our elders' elders—a storehouse of wisdom, *not fiction*. These are the stories so evocative, so beautifully imagined, that we've been telling them for centuries—*and that's a fact*.

Though most libraries have done away with a system so old-fashioned, books at the Woods Hole Library still get their due date stamped on slips stuck to the back page. This allows a librarian weeding the shelves to quickly glance at how many times a book has been checked out: Is it circulating? Is it worth keeping? The first date stamped on Molly Bang's masterfully illustrated re-telling of the Bengali folk tale "The Old Woman and the Red Pumpkin" is May 23, 1975. I hold the book, a book others held before I was born.

Past Plagues

March 2021

I vividly recall learning about the Black Death as a child. The thought of a bubonic plague wiping out whole medieval villages had both terrified and fascinated me. It felt like a demonic myth, so far in the past that it sat in my imagination beside Medusa and the Knights of the Round Table. My father, who took a certain relish in history's horrors, explained that the victim's festering lymph nodes swelled, turned bright red, then broke open. Half of Europe's inhabitants perished, he marveled. I tried to imagine what it would be like to have every other person I knew die.

Ellen Todd, a fellow member of my Unitarian-Universalist congregation, has been trying to imagine this: what would it be like to lose your mother, father, sister, husband, and two children all within two weeks of each other? That's what happened to her third great-grandmother, Mary Howard Affleck of Columbus, Ohio during the cholera outbreak of 1833. Nine months later, scarlet fever carried off Mary's two remaining children, including an infant, Harvey, conceived just prior to his father's death.

Ellen had delivered a moving guest sermon on the life of Mary Affleck this past Memorial Day, and the story of this woman's Job-scale suffering had stayed with me. Eventually I called Ellen to learn more. "It's so tragic," she told me. "There's no one left descended from her first husband. They all died. It's one of those dead ends in a family tree."

Cholera causes unrelenting vomiting and diarrhea; people die of dehydration within hours of falling ill. Mary Affleck's sister, Ann Howard, grew sick one afternoon, and by evening she was dead. A week later, Mary's father, Horton Howard, died. "He was taken with a violent relapse of cholera yesterday morning about six o'clock, and died about seven in the evening and was buried this morning at eight o clock," a family friend wrote to Horton's son-in-law. "He remained perfectly calm and sensible, and before the final close, expressed himself satisfied, and desired his love to all his friends."

On August 28, 1833, Jonathan Turner, a classics professor at Illinois College, wrote a letter to his fiancé describing the outbreak's devastation: "To meet a man at night and attend his funeral in the morning has ceased to alarm, much less to surprise. Some die in three hours, seldom do they live twelve, and very rarely twenty-four. As I have walked through the streets in the evening, I have seen through the windows and doors the sick and the dying, sometimes four or five in the same room in a log hut, some on the bed, others on the floor, and perhaps one or two sorrow-smitten beings crawling from bed to bed to give a cup of water or to brush away the flies."

Ellen's initial curiosity about her heritage ignited into "a quest" when she discovered a trove of her family's correspondence archived in the Dayton Metro Library in Ohio. Piecing together the story of Mary Affleck's life, Ellen felt amazed that she could have lived through such tragedy without succumbing to despair. After losing her first husband and their four children, Mary Affleck remarried, and it's this branch of the family tree from which Ellen is descended. A son from the second marriage was killed in the Civil War. "I was so sad for her," Ellen told me. "And yet also aware that my existence depends on the early deaths of these people."

Cholera is caused by the ingestion of fecal bacteria. In the nineteenth century, human waste was informally disposed of in streams or leaky cesspools. Modern water and sewage treatment systems have eliminated cholera's spread in the United States. But I was startled to learn that bubonic plague is still with us. In 2016, sixteen Americans caught the plague, and four of them died, according to the CDC. Certain rodent populations in the Western United States still carry the disease, and a bite from an infected flea—or skinning a rat without washing your hands—can pass the disease to humans. If it's caught early, antibiotics will clear the infection.

Darkness and Light

March 2021

On a cold but sunny day last week, I was walking along a dirt road; snow covered the shadowed parts of the road, but the sunny stretches had turned to mud, and I enjoyed stepping in the puddles with my boots, watching the sedimented water swirl in the sunshine. When I got back to the house, I saw an open patch of dirt near the front door; from it poked the tips of a half-dozen daffodils. I crouched and touched them gently with my fingers.

It's been a year since the governor first sent the state into lockdown. As of Wednesday, 12% of Americans have received at least one dose of the vaccine, and 5% have received both doses. I feel a little shock of joy (and a pang of envy) when someone tells me they've been vaccinated. Scientists are unsure what percentage of the population must be immune to COVID to stop the spread of the virus, and the percentage of the population that will refuse the vaccine is likewise unknown, but cautious optimism seems in order.

Last April, when our minister announced that services would be held online until May 2021, I'd scoffed at the ridiculously conservative forecast. *A whole year?* Was he purposely playing the doomsayer? Now I'd be surprised if we were back together that soon, or if Rory were able to play tag with his classmates when he enters first grade in the fall. So much joy and suffering, pain and pleasure, stems from contrast.

Let There Be Light

April 2021

Owing to my underlying condition of asthma, I got my first vaccine shot at the CVS in Plymouth this morning. I arrived in the parking lot an hour early and then waltzed in five minutes before 10:30 AM, bursting with good will, which the man checking me in returned in spades. (That must be a happy job, people stepping up to you all day giddy with gratitude and relief.) I took my vaccination card and stood in line in the greeting cards aisle. One of the birthday cards in the humor section had, "And God said, 'Let there be light'" in huge letters on the cover. I studied it, wondering what the punch line was.

"I can help the next person in line," a voice called from behind the white folding screen. A woman whose eyes matched the light blue of her disposable mask described the vaccine's side effects—fatigue, sore arm, perhaps flu-like symptoms—and then gently felt along my upper arm. "Relax."

My joy-induced endorphins must have masked the pain: I hardly felt a thing. The woman then instructed me to wait inside the store for fifteen minutes and come to her if I felt swelling in my throat. "We have EpiPens in case of anaphylactic shock," she said in a pleasant tone, patting a little bundle of wrapped syringes.

I got up and drifted away, passing the woman who'd been ahead of me in line. "I can't believe it," I said to her.

"I know; I feel like there should be music playing."

We made our way to the waiting chairs in the cosmetics aisle. It felt a bit like the first month of pregnancy: something tremendous was happening in my body, but without any visible signs to register the shift. Just sitting there felt exhilarating.

My mother had reached immunity the day before, and we'd hugged for the first time in over a year. When I got back to the car, I texted her a photo of my vaccination card. She texted back, "Welcome to the vaccinated."

Epilogue

November 2021

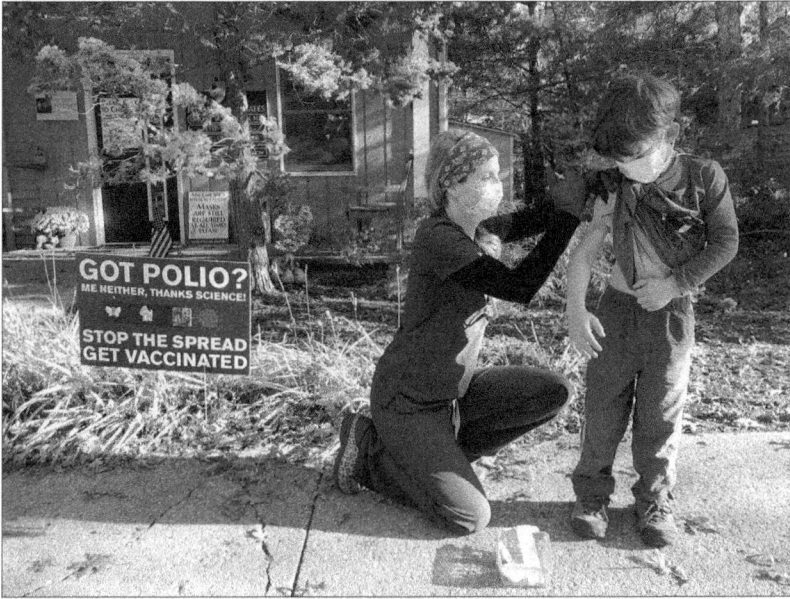

Rory received his first vaccine shot on November 9 at 2:17 in the afternoon. I'd failed to get a spot in the initial clinic held by his pediatrician's office. But when I called the following day, the nurse said they had three doses left over that would expire in an hour. Could I get him there in time?

About the Author

Elizabeth Saito has worked as a reporter for both the *Falmouth Enterprise* and *WCAI*, the Cape and Islands NPR station. In collaboration with The 300 Committee Land Trust, she is currently working on a trail guide to the con-

Photo © Kunio Saito

servation lands of Falmouth, Massachusetts. She can be reached at elizabeth.saito@gmail.com.

Photo © Mark Chester

About the Knob

A central character in this book, the Knob is a 13-acre spit of conservation land that shelters Quissett Harbor in Falmouth, Massachusetts. This wooded peninsula ends in a slender causeway that leads up to a pinnacle with views of Buzzards Bay. The property was willed to the Salt Pond Areas Bird Sanctuaries land trust in 1973 by Cornelia Carey. Its 0.8-mile shoreline is a mix of rocky and sandy beach as well as extensive stone armament that the Quissett Harbor Preservation Trust pays millions of dollars to maintain against the forces of erosion.

Additional copies of this book can be purchased at Eight Cousins bookstore at 189 Main Street in Falmouth, MA or online at eightcousins.com

www.ingramcontent.com/pod-product-compliance
Lightning Source LLC
Chambersburg PA
CBHW030251030426
42336CB00009B/341